VIRTUAL FIELD TRIPS

THE
ALAMO

A MyReportLinks.com Book

Wim Coleman and Pat Perrin

MyReportLinks.com Books

an imprint of

 Ensiow Publishers, Inc.
Box 398, 40 Industrial Road
Berkeley Heights, NJ 07922
USA

MyReportLinks.com Books, an imprint of Enslow Publishers, Inc. MyReportLinks®
is a registered trademark of Enslow Publishers, Inc.

Library of Congress Cataloging-in-Publication Data

Coleman, Wim.
  The Alamo / Wim Coleman and Pat Perrin.
    p. cm. — (Virtual field trips)
  Includes bibliographical references and index.
  ISBN 0-7660-5221-4
  1. Alamo (San Antonio, Tex.)—Siege, 1836—Juvenile literature. 2. Alamo (San Antonio, Tex.)—Juvenile
literature. I. Perrin, Pat. II. Title. III. Series.
  F390.C68 2005
  976.4'03—dc22
                              2004006590

Printed in the United States of America

10 9 8 7 6 5 4 3 2 1

To Our Readers:
Through the purchase of this book, you and your library gain access to the Report Links that specifically back
up this book.
The Publisher will provide access to the Report Links that back up this book and will keep these Report Links
up to date on **www.myreportlinks.com** for five years from the book's first publication date.
We have done our best to make sure all Internet addresses in this book were active and appropriate when we went
to press. However, the author and the Publisher have no control over, and assume no liability for, the material
available on those Internet sites or on other Web sites they may link to.
The usage of the MyReportLinks.com Books Web site is subject to the terms and conditions stated on the Usage
Policy Statement on **www.myreportlinks.com**.
A password may be required to access the Report Links that back up this book. The password is found on the
bottom of page 4 of this book.
Any comments or suggestions can be sent by e-mail to comments@myreportlinks.com or to the address on the
back cover.

MyReportLinks.com Books
Great Books, Great Links, Great for Research!

The Internet sites listed on the next four pages can save you hours of research time. These Internet sites—we call them "Report Links"—are constantly changing, but we keep them up to date on our Web site.

Give it a try! Type http://www.myreportlinks.com into your browser, click on the series title, then the book title, and scroll down to the Report Links listed for this book.

The Report Links will bring you to great source documents, photographs, and illustrations. MyReportLinks.com Books save you time, feature Report Links that are kept up to date, and make report writing easier than ever!

Please see "To Our Readers" on the copyright page for important information about this book, the MyReportLinks.com Web site, and the Report Links that back up this book.

Please enter **FTA1531** if asked for a password.

Report Links

The Internet sites described below can be accessed at
http://www.myreportlinks.com

▶**The Alamo**   *EDITOR'S CHOICE

Extensive overview of the Alamo, including biographies of the people
who defended the Alamo, and a virtual walking tour of the site.
Information for teachers is also included.

▶**Remember the Alamo**   *EDITOR'S CHOICE

Learn more about the men who fought at the Alamo. They are brought
to life through a series of biographies and images. You can also read
survivor stories.

▶**Alamo, Battle of the**   *EDITOR'S CHOICE

As many as 257 people died facing the Mexican Army while defending
the Alamo against its final assault. Six hundred Mexicans were said to
have perished. Become familiar with the details of this famous battle.

▶**Alamo Images: Changing Perceptions of
a Texas Experience**   *EDITOR'S CHOICE

The thirteen-day siege of the Alamo was a pivotal episode in the history
of Texas. Survivor accounts of the battle acted as the basis for some of
the earliest paintings and depictions. Maps are included.

▶**Antonio López de Santa Anna**   *EDITOR'S CHOICE

General Antonio López de Santa Anna was elected president of Mexico
in 1833. He had led Mexico to freedom by fighting against the Spanish
Conquistadors. Learn more about his life.

▶**Battle of the Alamo**   *EDITOR'S CHOICE

You will learn the early history of the Alamo. Read about what
happened before, during, and in the days after the battle. There is also
a list of names of those who lost their lives at the Alamo.

Report Links

The Internet sites described below can be accessed at
http://www.myreportlinks.com

▶The Alamo: Documenting Courage

A short and easy to understand summary of the battle that took place at the Alamo, a fort that was originally a mission set up by Spanish priests. Learn the details of a battle that changed the history of Texas.

▶Alamo Cenotaph

The Texas Centennial Commission erected the Alamo Cenotaph in front of the Alamo in San Antonio. Made of gray Georgia marble and pink Texas granite, the memorial rises 60 feet from its base and is 40 feet long and 12 feet wide.

▶Alamo Noncombatants

Learn what happened to some of the most famous survivors of the Alamo. Find out who they were and what they did with their lives after the battle.

▶Antonio López de Santa Anna: Sons of DeWitt Colony

General Antonio López de Santa Anna lived to the age of eighty-four after fighting in more battles than Napoleon and George Washington combined. He ruled Mexico eleven times as president and dictator. Read more about his character, courage, and ideas.

▶Daughters of the Republic of Texas Library

The memory and spirit of those who fought for the independence of Texas is maintained by the Daughters of the Republic of Texas and its library. The organization encourages historical research, preserves documents and relics, and conserves historic locations, such as the Alamo.

▶David Crockett: His Life and Adventures

This site covers David Crockett's life, including his early childhood, youthful adventures, and marriage. Learn more about this extraordinary man and how he died at the Alamo.

▶*The Fall of the Alamo*

This narrative was written in 1860 by Captain R. M. Potter, who lived near the Alamo at the time it fell. It was first published in the *San Antonio Herald* and later distributed extensively as a pamphlet.

▶Houston, Samuel

Born in Virginia, Samuel Houston became one of the most important figures in the history of Texas, defeating Mexican General Santa Anna at the Battle of San Jacinto. Learn about Houston's life, including how he once lived among the Cherokee.

Any comments? Contact us: **comments@myreportlinks.com**

Report Links

The Internet sites described below can be accessed at http://www.myreportlinks.com

▶James Bowie

Fearless and bold, James Bowie had a reputation for being an expert at handling a knife. He grew up in Kentucky and Louisiana and died at the Alamo. Learn more about Bowie at this Web site.

▶José Antonio Navarro

José Antonio Navarro was a staunch supporter of Texas independence. He was elected to the Congress of the Republic of Texas and was a very close friend of Stephen Austin, one of the founders of the republic. Some of the letters exchanged by them are included.

▶Republic of Texas Money

The Republic of Texas authorized its first currency in the fall of 1837. The common name for it was "Star Money" because of the star printed on the bill. Learn more about "Star Money" and other bills.

▶Sam Houston Memorial Museum

Educational programs, fun stuff for kids, virtual tours, photo albums of the Houston family, and biographical information are just some of the areas covered at this Web site. Learn more about the life and times of General Sam Houston.

▶San Antonio De Valero Mission

Learn the early history of the San Antonio De Valero Mission, which was founded by Father Antonio de San Buenaventura y Olivares of Spain. This mission was the site for the Battle of the Alamo.

▶San Jacinto Battle Report: Transcript

Read the actual transcript of the letter that General Sam Houston wrote to D. G. Burnett, the president of the Republic of Texas, after the Battle of San Jacinto. This battle ended Mexican control over Texas.

▶San Jacinto Museum of History

General Antonio López de Santa Anna of Mexico and his army faced Sam Houston and his Texas revolutionaries on April 21, 1836. The Mexicans were awakening from their afternoon siesta when Houston ordered the attack. Learn more about the famous Battle of San Jacinto.

▶Sons of DeWitt Colony, Texas

The DeWitt Colony of Texas played an important role in the early stages of resistance against Mexican dictatorship that eventually led to the independence of Texas.

Report Links

▶**Susanna Dickenson (Dickinson)**

Biographical sketch of Susanna Dickenson, who lived through the terror of the Alamo. She lost her husband during the battle and was shot in the leg. After the siege ended, Mexican General Santa Anna spared her life and used her as a courier.

▶**The Tejano Association for Historical Preservation**

This group was formed to identify and preserve historical buildings and sites with significance to the Hispanic-American, early Texan, French, and native/indigenous cultures. Learn about some of the more famous Tejanos and why it is important to preserve their memory.

▶**Texans Buy Controversial Diary That Challenges Alamo Legend**

Read more about the mystery that surrounds the death of David Crockett. Did he die fighting at the Alamo, or was he executed by Santa Anna afterward? Learn more about the controversy and how the experts are debating it.

▶**Texas: The Lone Star State**

Read about the history, geography, and culture of Texas as well as its fight for independence. The biggest state in the continental United States, Texas had a unique beginning. Learn more about it.

▶**Texas Historic Sites Atlas**

Using a database of 238,000 historical and archeological site records documenting Texas history, the atlas allows you to find information on historic sites and their condition. Use it to search for the Alamo.

▶**Texian Legacy Association**

Researching, preserving, and teaching others about the culture and history of pre-1840 Texas, this association works with schools and the public. They utilize interactive reenactments, presentations, and demonstrations. Includes lots of articles.

▶**Travis, William Barret**

Born in South Carolina, Travis became one of the most heroic figures in the history of Texas, defending the Alamo against Mexican General Santa Anna and his army. Learn about Travis's life as a lawyer and how he ended up dying at the Alamo.

▶**The University of Texas Institute of Texan Cultures at San Antonio**

School outreach programs, exhibitions, educational resource kits, historical photo collections, and publications are just some of the ways that the Institute of Texan Cultures preserves and teaches us about the cultural history of Texas. Lots of information on the Alamo is included on this Web site.

Alamo Facts

 The Alamo museum and shrine, is located at 300 Alamo Plaza in downtown San Antonio, Texas.

 More than 2.5 million people visit the Alamo each year.

 Alamo Plaza is a park-like, 4.2-acre site owned by the state of Texas. It contains some original Alamo buildings, new buildings and park areas, and exhibits to help visitors learn about the famous Battle of the Alamo.

 The Alamo museum and shrine is managed by the Daughters of the Republic of Texas (DRT), an organization that preserves historical records and places. The DRT keeps the Alamo open to visitors, and the admission is free.

 Most pictures of the Alamo show the church with the curved top that is on the site now. At the time of the famous Battle of the Alamo, though, the church did not look like that at all because it had not been completed.

 We remember the Alamo as the scene of a very bloody nineteenth-century battle. It was actually built as an early eighteenth-century Spanish mission—a place where priests could convert native Indians to Christianity.

 The word *Alamo* means "cottonwood," a kind of tree.

The name *Texas* comes from a Caddo American Indian word, *tejas,* meaning "friends" or "allies."

 *A map of Texas* ▷

A Desperate Dash for Help

One winter night in 1836, a cold north wind blew across the San Antonio River valley in Texas. Two men on horseback slipped through the darkness, hoping they would not be seen. The riders, though, had to pass near an enemy camp. Would they be captured? Would their mission fail before it really got started?

▶ The Dark and Dangerous Ride

One of the men was Captain Juan Nepomuceno Seguín. His fellow soldiers had voted for Seguín to make this ride. The second

△ An image of the front of the Alamo at night. On the night of February 29, 1836, Captain Seguín and Antonio Cruz y Arocha sneaked out to see how far the Mexican Army had advanced.

man was Antonio Cruz y Arocha, Seguín's aide. Seguín and Arocha were revolutionaries, fighting for Texas independence.

On that night of February 29, 1836, Seguín and Arocha were sneaking through enemy lines. Seguín later wrote, "we left at eight o'clock at night after having bid good-bye to all my comrades, expecting certain death."[1] Behind them, those comrades were trying to defend themselves in an old and crumbling fort known as the Alamo. They could not hold out for long.

According to some stories, Seguín was on a borrowed horse, loaned to him by the famous knife-fighting frontiersman, Jim Bowie. By that time, Bowie—who was back in the Alamo—was very ill, and in no condition to ride a horse.[2]

Spotted by the Enemy

Seguín and Arocha knew that a company of enemy Mexican cavalry was stationed nearby. Fortunately, the cavalrymen were not mounted on their horses. They were getting ready to rest for the night.

The Mexicans, though, had posted guards around the camp. One of those watchmen spotted the two riders. The guard called out to them.

Seguín replied in Spanish, "We are countrymen."[3] He and Arocha pretended to be local ranchers going home.[4] Apparently the guard believed that—at first.

Seguín and Arocha rode closer to the watchman. Just when they were near enough for the man to get a good look at them, Seguín and Arocha spurred their horses and charged past. Shots rang out, but the riders escaped. Seguín's Spanish had bought them enough time to make their getaway.[5]

Texans in Revolt

Seguín, Arocha, and the enemy guard were all Mexicans. At that time, Texas was part of Mexico. Juan Seguín had grown up on a

General Antonio López de Santa Anna led the Mexican Army against the Alamo's defenders. Santa Anna served as president of Mexico eleven times.

large, nearby ranch. His father, Don Erasmo Seguín, had been active in the local government. As a young professional following in his father's footsteps, Juan Seguín also held several political offices, including mayor and postmaster.

The Seguíns, like many others who lived in Texas, had grown troubled over the Mexican government. They did not like what was happening in Mexico City, the faraway capital of Mexico.

The Mexican Constitution of 1824 guaranteed the people a wide range of rights. However, Mexican president Antonio López de Santa Anna had discarded that constitution. President Santa Anna had been elected to his office by the National Congress. Soon he decided that his country was not ready for democracy, and he proclaimed himself dictator of Mexico.[6]

Juan Seguín had joined the Texas Revolution because he saw Santa Anna as a threat to freedom. He had raised a company of thirty-seven men to serve with him.

Like all of those who rebelled against Santa Anna, Seguín knew there would be no going back. If Texas lost this conflict, the rebels would be considered traitors to Mexico. They would surely pay with their lives.

▷ The End of the Ride

Seguín and Arocha were looking for more men to come and help them defend the Alamo. They rode through the night to the Texas town of Goliad. There, Seguín discovered that a group of Texans had already left to help out at the Alamo, but their wagons had broken down.[7] They also had heard that Santa Anna's soldiers were headed toward Goliad.

Seguín continued on his way to find Sam Houston, major general of the Texas Revolution. Seguín organized another company of soldiers that served as the rear guard to Houston's army. This meant that Seguín's troops would protect Houston's troops from being attacked from behind.

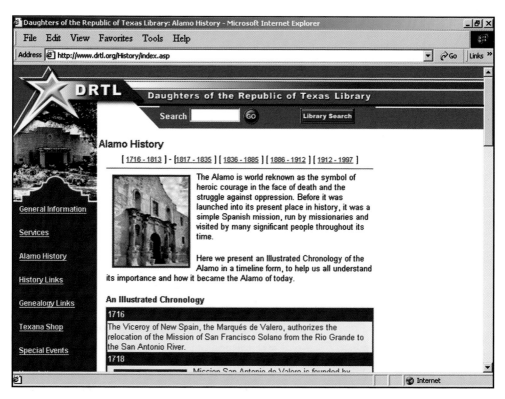

▲ The Daughters of the Republic of Texas was founded in 1891 to carry on the spirit and memory of those who fought for the independence of Texas. The organization runs the Alamo museum, Shrine, and gift shop.

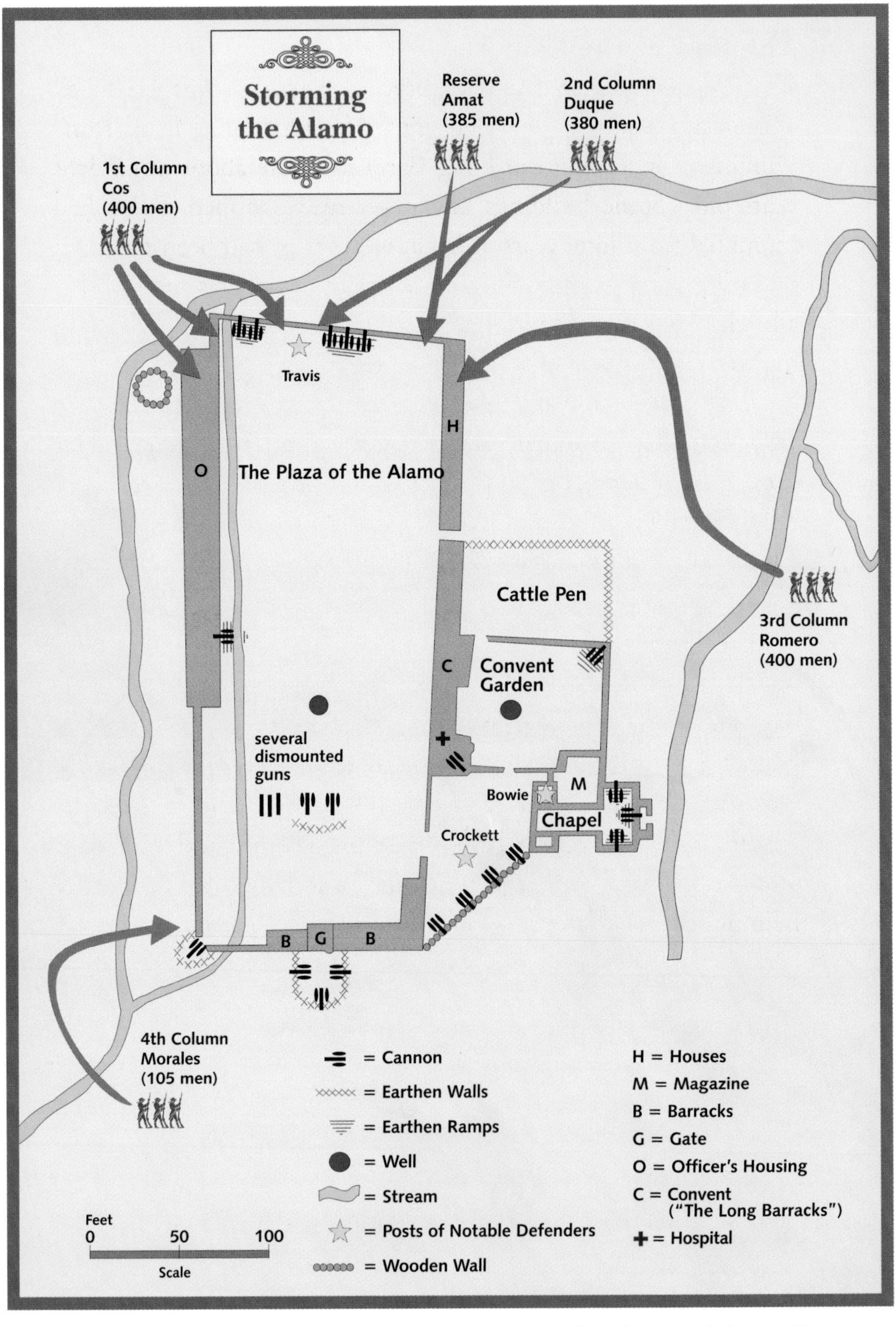

Storming the Alamo

Reserve Amat (385 men)

2nd Column Duque (380 men)

1st Column Cos (400 men)

Travis

H

O

The Plaza of the Alamo

Cattle Pen

C

Convent Garden

3rd Column Romero (400 men)

several dismounted guns

Bowie

M

Chapel

Crockett

B G B

4th Column Morales (105 men)

= Cannon

= Earthen Walls

= Earthen Ramps

= Well

= Stream

= Posts of Notable Defenders

= Wooden Wall

H = Houses

M = Magazine

B = Barracks

G = Gate

O = Officer's Housing

C = Convent ("The Long Barracks")

+ = Hospital

Feet
0   50   100

Scale

▲ This map shows Santa Anna's plans for storming the Alamo and the positions taken by the Alamo's defenders.

The Fortress That Fell

By 1836, the Alamo had been used as a Spanish mission called Misión San Antonio de Valero and a fortress. Some of its stone buildings—including the Long Barrack—were about a hundred years old.[8] Some buildings had never been finished. Some had crumbled from long years of harsh weather or had been damaged by earlier battles. The walls around much of the area were adobe, a brick-like material made of sun-dried earth and straw.[9] Some of the walls were made of stone.

The old mission did not make a very strong fortress. Those who defended it were badly outnumbered. As anyone might expect, the Alamo fell. Soon, "Remember the Alamo!" became a rallying cry for the Texas Army fighting for independence from Mexico. The spirit of the Alamo helped shape the Southwestern United States.

Visiting the Alamo

The site of the Alamo represents the great sacrifice its defenders made for the sake of freedom. In downtown San Antonio, Texas, visitors to Alamo Plaza can see where that battle took place. Alamo Plaza and the Alamo museum, shrine, and gift shop include some of the original buildings and many exhibits that help us appreciate the spirit of those who died there.

Land of Many Flags

The first people who lived in the large area we know as Texas were American Indians—Comanche, Apache, Caddo, and members of other tribes. In the 1540s, explorers from Spain reached that part of the New World. The Spaniards met the Caddo tribe and picked up their word *tejas,* a greeting that meant "friends" or "allies." The Mexican state was named Tejas, and it later became the state of Texas.

Over the years, six different national flags have flown over Texas. First, there was the Spanish flag after Spain claimed the land in the 1500s. Between 1685 and 1690, the French flag waved over a part of eastern Texas claimed by that nation. By 1690, France had abandoned most of its settlements. Present-day northern Texas was purchased by the United States in the Louisiana Purchase. The Mexican flag was raised after Mexico won its independence from Spain in 1821.

In 1836, Texas won independence from Mexico and became an independent republic. (In a republic, the people elect representatives to their government.) The Republic of Texas flew the "Lone Star" flag.

◁ The defenders of the Alamo did not die in vain. In 1845, the Republic of Texas won independence from Mexico. This is now the Texas state flag. It is based on the "Lone Star" flag that flew during the Siege of Béxar.

▲ *This image shows the hallway of the Long Barrack as it appeared in 1936. This was the building where the defenders of the Alamo slept.*

In 1845, the Republic of Texas was annexed by the United States as the twenty-eighth state. Since then, the United States flag has flown over Texas except during the Civil War. During that time, Texans flew the flag of the Confederate States of America.

Spanish Explorers and Conquistadors

In 1492, explorer Christopher Columbus came across some islands that he thought must be the Indies (India and nearby areas). Those islands turned out to be a part of the world Europeans had never seen before.

In 1493, the powerful Roman Catholic pope granted the lands that Columbus had discovered to Spain. After a dispute with Portugal, Spain received the right to explore most of these lands when the Treaty of Tordesillas was signed in 1494. Popular legends of that time told of cities made of gold and jewels. These were called the Cities of Cíbola. Spanish explorers followed those legends to the New World. They never found these cities of gold, but some did get rich.

Spanish military men called conquistadors defeated the Aztec Indian nation in central Mexico. Gold taken from the Aztecs helped make Spain the world's most powerful country for a time. The conquistadors also explored present-day Florida, the Southwestern United States, and California. They claimed those lands for Spain, but they found no gold in them. The whole area north of the river we call the Rio Grande was a disappointment to the Spanish. They kept it, but only as a protective buffer for their holdings in Mexico.

Spanish Missions

When the pope approved the Treaty of Tordesillas, he gave the explorers a special responsibility. They were to convert the natives to Christianity. So most Spanish ships brought along priests in addition to conquistadors. The priests built missions—places where they could teach the natives.

Spanish settlers also came to the New World. Settlements grew up near the missions as conquistadors married native women. These settlements and missions were protected by soldiers in nearby forts called presidios.

The Mission That Became the Alamo

In the spring of 1718, Father Antonio de San Buenaventura y Olivares founded the mission of San Antonio de Valero on the east bank of the San Antonio River. The town of Béxar rose up nearby, as fifteen families from the Canary Islands moved there. The San Antonio de Béxar Presidio was built to protect the town and mission. In 1724, the mission was moved to its present location on the west bank of the river.

The town of Béxar became known as San Antonio Béxar. In the mid-1800s the town became simply called San Antonio.[1]

The Long Barrack

The first buildings completed in the mission were probably made of adobe. They did not last long. In 1724, work started on the *convento,* a home for the priests. Finished in 1744, the convento was a two-story stone building with offices, kitchens, dining rooms, sleeping quarters, and guest rooms. Later, the building housed soldiers and was known as the Long Barrack.

In 1805, the Spanish governor of Texas, Manuel Antonio Cordero y Bustamante, turned the upstairs of the Long Barrack into a hospital—the first in Texas. Today, the remains of this early building are part of the Long Barrack Museum at the Alamo.[2] Among the exhibits, visitors can see surgical instruments from the 1800s and a hospital ward set up as it would have been in the early 1800s.

▲ *This side of the building is the front of the church, or chapel, at the Alamo. Before becoming a fort, the Alamo was a Spanish mission called Misión San Antonio de Valero.*

The Church

In 1744, work began on a stone church. Unfortunately, this building collapsed by 1756. Two years later, construction began on the present church. Today, it has a high, curved top above its doorway. Most people think of this building as the Alamo.

The mission church did not originally look like it does today. The plan was to have a bell tower on each side of the doorway. Inside was to be a large space with grand arches and a dome. Over the years, work slowed down. The roof of the church was never finished, and some of the construction crumbled.[3]

By the time of the Battle of the Alamo, the church was roofless. Its walls had been damaged in earlier fighting.[4] Even before the famous battle, the church looked like an old ruin.

The Mission Becomes a Military Fortress

In 1793, Spanish officials decided to close a number of Texas missions. For quite some time, the mission of San Antonio de Valero was abandoned except for a handful of American Indians who had stayed after the mission closed. The adobe walls suffered from neglect.[5]

In the early 1800s, the Spanish stationed a cavalry unit at the old mission. The unit—the Second Flying Company from San Carlos de Alamo de Parras—called their headquarters the "Alamo."[6] The Spanish word *alamo* means "cottonwood," a type

of tree. Later, cottonwoods were planted along a stretch of road through Béxar. Yet

An antique cannon displayed at the Alamo.

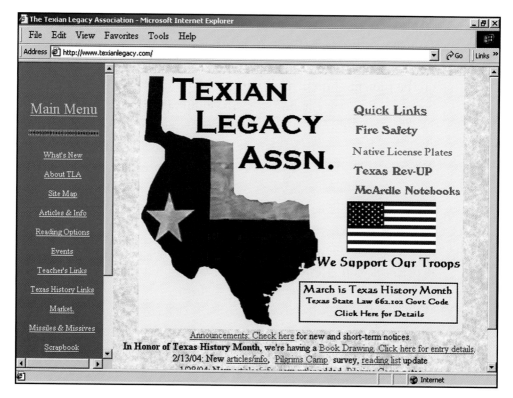

The Texian Legacy Association is committed to the preservation of Texas's history prior to 1840, including the African-American, American Indian, Hispanic-American, and pioneer perspectives, cultures, and lifestyles.

the name was used for the fort long before that road existed. The Alamo Company, a company of one hundred soldiers, named it for their own hometown.[7]

United States Immigrants in Texas

Very few Mexicans moved into Texas. Mexico City, the center of Mexican culture, was too far away. On the other hand, Texas was attractive to some citizens of the neighboring United States.

In the 1800s, the prospect of cheap land drew settlers from the United States in large numbers. To live in Texas, these immigrants had to become Mexican citizens. They were supposed to join the Catholic Church, though many simply pretended to. Many settlers learned to speak Spanish in addition to their native English. By the 1830s, the Mexican government became alarmed at the number of United States citizens who had moved into Texas. Mexico was afraid that the settlers wanted to add Texas to the United States.

Tejanos and Texians

Texas was part of Mexico when the Battle of the Alamo took place. People of Spanish descent who were born in Texas or lived there often called themselves Tejanos. They had built the churches, towns, and ranches of early Texas. Many of them felt no strong connection with faraway central Mexico.[8]

Immigrants to Texas from the United States and elsewhere referred to themselves as Texians. Some Texians thought that Texas should be a separate nation, because of their differences with the Mexican government. Others believed that, sooner or later, Texas would become part of the United States. Still other Texians were content with the region belonging to Mexico—as long as the Mexican government did not interfere with their rights.

When Mexico became a republic in 1824, Texas was made part of the state of Coahuila. The state capital was then moved from San Antonio de Béxar to farther-away Saltillo, and Texas citizens began to protest. They felt that Texas should be a separate state of Mexico.

Their protests increased when President Santa Anna discarded the Mexican Constitution in 1834. Tejanos, for the most part, simply wanted to restore the constitution, while most Texians had wanted independence or statehood. However, Tejanos and Texians shared a desire to be rid of the Mexican dictator, Santa Anna.

Famous Soldiers

In September 1835, Texas asked the Mexican government for separate statehood. In response, Mexican president Santa Anna sent General Martín Perfecto de Cós and his troops to Béxar. Their orders were to disarm the Texians and restore order.

General Cós put San Antonio de Béxar under military rule. In response, the Texas rebels fiercely attacked the Mexican Army. Cós soon surrendered the town and the Alamo, leaving the weapons in the fort to the rebels.[1]

Mexico's President Santa Anna was furious when he heard about the surrender.

▶ Antonio López de Santa Anna

Santa Anna had become a soldier at the age of sixteen. He was wounded in the hand by an Indian arrow while still a teenager.[2] He became a general at twenty-seven. Nobody doubted his courage, but Santa Anna was also vain and treacherous.

During the Mexican War for Independence (1810–21), Santa Anna first fought on Spain's side. When Mexican rebels offered him a higher military rank, Santa Anna switched sides.[3] When Mexico won its independence from Spain, Santa Anna claimed more than his share of the credit, calling himself the "Napoleon of the West."[4]

In 1833, Santa Anna was elected president of Mexico. In 1834, he declared himself Mexico's absolute dictator.[5] Santa Anna's policies were the main reason that Texas rebelled against Mexico. When General Cós surrendered Béxar to the Texians, Santa Anna decided to put down the Texas Revolution personally.

Santa Anna led his army northward, determined to throw all foreigners out of Texas. As the word got around, an unusual group of characters assembled at the Alamo to join the fight for Texas.

Jim Bowie

Jim Bowie was a true frontier legend. He was at least six feet tall, with piercing gray eyes and a fierce temper. An outdoorsman from his youth in Louisiana and Kentucky, Bowie enjoyed capturing horses, deer, and wild cattle with a lasso. He was also said to have ridden alligators for sport.

Like many living legends, Bowie was both a scoundrel and hero. Before settling in Texas, he smuggled slaves. Even though the U.S. Congress had made it illegal to ship slaves from Africa, Bowie bought Africans from pirates and sold them to slave owners. He was also known to sell land that was not legally his.[6]

In 1827, Bowie was involved in a brawl that broke out during a duel between two other men. Bowie suffered two bullet wounds

and many knife wounds—but managed to kill an enemy with a large butcher knife. Both the killing and the "Bowie knife" became famous. In the early 1830s, Bowie settled in Texas and married a wealthy young

Jim Bowie was a famous frontiersman and soldier. Bowie was originally elected to lead the volunteer fighters at the Alamo, but he fell ill and was confined to a bed.

Mexican woman. She was the daughter of the future governor of Coahuila y Tejas.

Bowie's legend as a fighter grew during his first few years in Texas. He joined a revolutionary group called the War Party to fight for Texas independence. The commander of the rebel forces was General Sam Houston. In January 1836, Houston sent Colonel Bowie and twenty-five men to the Alamo. The general wanted Bowie to destroy the Alamo fortifications, to make it useless to the enemy. Bowie and his men were supposed to remove the Alamo's twenty-four cannon from the fort and then move them eastward.

Bowie did not have the oxen, mules, or horses needed to move the artillery. He decided to reinforce the Alamo instead. Then, in February, another officer arrived to take command at the Alamo—William Travis. Bowie was elected to be the commander of the volunteer soldiers while Travis was elected commander of the regular army. On February 24, Bowie collapsed from a mysterious illness. Today's historians generally believe he suffered from either pneumonia or tuberculosis.[7] Jim Bowie was too sick to fight, and he soon gave up command to Travis.

William B. Travis

Lieutenant Colonel William B. Travis was only twenty-six years old at the time of the Battle of the Alamo. He was impressive and tall, with blue eyes and reddish-brown hair. He was also very sure of himself—even somewhat reckless and impatient.[8]

Travis was born in South Carolina and grew up in Alabama, where he was a teacher, lawyer, and newspaper publisher. He also joined the Alabama Militia. When he was nineteen, Travis married a sixteen-year-old girl and together they had two children. In 1831, Travis mysteriously left Alabama, abandoning his wife, son, and unborn daughter. It has been said that he left because he thought that his wife had been unfaithful to him. It is perhaps more likely that he left because of debts and business problems.[9]

William Barret Travis was the commander in charge at the Alamo. Travis was known as a courageous risk taker.

When he arrived in Texas, Travis became involved in the Texians' quarrels with the Mexican government. He soon joined the War Party of Texians who were determined to fight for Texas independence. He helped the Texians prepare for the Siege of Béxar in which the Texians gained control of San Antonio, but he left for San Felipe before the battle took place. In February 1836, Travis took command of Béxar and the Alamo. His job was to defend the town and fortress against recapture by the Mexicans.

David Crockett

By the time of Bowie's collapse, another famous frontiersman had arrived at the Alamo. David Crockett's frontier adventures began during his childhood in Tennessee. When he was only ten years old, his father hired him out to a cattle herder, who kidnapped him. Young David escaped and made his way more than a hundred miles home.[10]

With only about six months of formal schooling, David Crockett learned most of what he knew from the wilderness.[11] He was said to have killed 105 bears in one year alone. He fought in battles against the American Indians, serving in the Creek Indian War of 1813 under the future president Andrew Jackson.[12]

David Crockett's real-life adventures were often stranger than the legends told about him. He courted his first wife, Polly

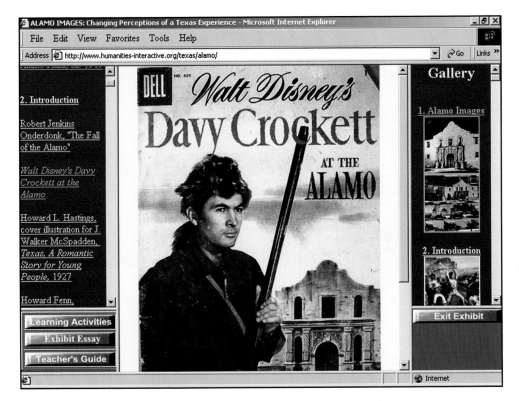

ALAMO IMAGES: Changing Perceptions of a Texas Experience - Microsoft Internet Explorer

File   Edit   View   Favorites   Tools   Help

Address   http://www.humanities-interactive.org/texas/alamo/   Go   Links »

▲ *Walt Disney recognized David "Davy" Crockett as a symbol of the American frontier. Disney aired five episodes of a show based on the life and times of Davy Crockett. They also created the 1955* Davy Crockett at the Alamo *comic book (shown here).*

Finley, after rescuing her from being lost in the woods.[13] He also cheated death more than once. Crockett suffered from malaria while exploring Alabama in 1815 and was reported dead to his family. His children and his second wife, Elizabeth Patton, were greatly relieved when he arrived home after all. He also barely survived a Mississippi River boat wreck in 1826.[14]

David Crockett entered politics in 1821. Despite his lack of education, Crockett was always ready with a clever riddle or an entertaining story. He was not above winning votes by passing out tobacco and liquor.

▲ *Henry McArdle's painting* Dawn at the Alamo, *created in 1905.*

Crockett was elected to the United States Congress in 1827. Unfortunately, he made a dangerous political enemy out of his former commander, President Andrew Jackson. Crockett refused to support Jackson's policies toward American Indians because he thought they were cruel. Crockett was voted out of Congress for good in 1835.

Crockett was then forty-nine years old and had been voted out of political office. At a farewell gathering in Memphis, he told his fellow Tennesseeans, "You may all go to hell and I will go to Texas." He left for Texas the very next day.

He fell in love with living in Texas and hoped to move his family there. "I am rejoiced at my fate," he wrote on January 9, 1836. This was the last letter he wrote before his death.[15]

On February 8, he arrived in Béxar with a band of volunteers. He had no intention of stealing any thunder from Bowie or Travis. Instead, he asked simply to serve in the Alamo's defense as a "high private."[16]

David Crockett was eager for a fight, and an army of Mexicans was on its way.

Chapter 4

The Siege and Battle of the Alamo

On Tuesday, February 23, 1836, a Texian soldier in Béxar's church tower caught a glimpse of an approaching army.[1] It was not reinforcements for the Alamo. It was Santa Anna and about 1,500 Mexican soldiers—on their way to attack. Travis had not expected the Mexican Army to arrive until the middle of March. Santa Anna had pushed his troops hard on that furious march north.

Travis quickly ordered his soldiers into the Alamo compound.[2] They were joined by a few civilians, including wives and

▲ *This diorama of the siege at the Alamo re-creates the battle scene as it may have appeared from survivors and historians' accounts. You can see where soldiers took their positions to defend from on top of the mission walls.*

children of soldiers, and several slaves. The gravely ill Jim Bowie gathered provisions in Béxar. He herded some twenty or thirty cattle into the compound and also gathered eighty or ninety bushels of corn.[3] The defenders and their families had enough to eat for several weeks, perhaps even a month. They had plenty of guns and cannon, bullets, and cannonballs.

At the news of Santa Anna's approach, most of Béxar's population fled. The town was almost empty. Santa Anna arrived in the Béxar town square and ordered a red flag raised on the church tower.

Those in the Alamo knew what the blood-red flag meant: "Surrender. We will take no prisoners."

Colonel William Travis boldly replied with the symbolic boom of a cannon.[4]

▶ The Hope That Help Would Come

The Alamo was designed to be a mission, not a fortress. It sprawled across some three acres (130,680 square feet)—much too large an area for fewer than two hundred soldiers to defend. The Alamo's adobe and stone outer walls were too weak to withstand much cannon fire. During the siege, men in the compound had to keep piling dirt against the walls to keep them from collapsing.[5]

Still, the Texans had at least one reason to remain hopeful. Travis and his soldiers were confident that more soldiers would soon join them. Colonel James Walker Fannin was about one hundred miles away from Béxar. He was expected to bring more than three hundred Texian soldiers to the Alamo's defense.

Unfortunately, Fannin and his soldiers suffered one delay after another. Fannin was held up by a broken wagon, a lack of food, and other difficulties. His promised forces never reached the Alamo.[6]

Travis sent message after message—including the one carried by Juan Seguín—to the commanders of the Texas Revolution. On the second day of the siege, Travis ended a message with his immortal battle cry, "Victory or Death."

A group of thirty-two volunteers from Gonzales arrived on March 1, 1836. Although the Alamo's defenders were cheered by the help, Travis knew that he needed at least ten times that many men.[7]

Cannon Balls, Rifle Fire, and Dueling Musicians

By the ninth day of the siege, Santa Anna had fired some two hundred cannon balls into the fort.[8] The defenders fired their cannon, too. One shot destroyed Santa Anna's headquarters, but the Mexican leader was not inside. Not a single Texian was killed or injured during the first twelve days. On the other hand, the Texian riflemen firing from the Alamo walls killed many Mexican soldiers.[9]

Santa Anna also attacked with music. He had his band play Mexican military tunes, hoping to impress—and perhaps depress—the defenders.

▲ This engraving shows the Texian flag flying high above the Alamo as the Mexican troops gathered outside to begin their attack.

Inside the Alamo, legend has it that Davy Crockett raised morale with jokes, stories, and his famous fiddle. John McGregor, a Scotsman, played his bagpipes. According to legend, they had contests to see who could play louder—Crockett on his fiddle or McGregor on his bagpipes. It has been said that they both did their best to drown out Santa Anna's band.[10]

The Line in the Sand

March 5 was the twelfth day of the siege. More of Santa Anna's military had arrived, bringing his army to about 2,400 men. According to traditional estimates, there were still only 189 defenders inside the Alamo.[11]

A Frenchman named Louis Rose said that Travis gave his men one last chance to escape with their lives. He supposedly drew a line in the sand with his sword. Then he asked all those willing to stay and die to walk across it. Jim Bowie was too ill to rise from his bed. So Bowie asked several men to carry the bed across the line.[12]

Louis Rose refused to cross the line. He was allowed to leave the fort, and he lived to tell others about the first twelve days of the siege.[13] All the other men joined Travis.

Attack Before Dawn

At five o'clock the next morning, the Texians inside the Alamo were awakened by a horrifying sound. Santa Anna's buglers were playing the *Degüello*—a signal to cut the defenders' throats.[14] The final attack was beginning. No prisoners would be taken.

Colonel Travis ran through the compound, shouting, "Come on boys, the Mexicans are upon us and we'll give them Hell!"[15]

About 1,800 Mexican troops advanced toward the fort.[16] Many were cut down immediately by Alamo cannons, but many more kept coming.

The Mexicans thrust ladders against the fort's walls and began climbing. With rifles and muskets, the defenders gunned them down. The attackers showed just as much courage as the Alamo's defenders. Wave after wave of them were killed, but still they came. Finally, Santa Anna's soldiers poured over the walls and into the compound.

Travis stood atop the crumbling northern wall. He was among the first Texians to die, from a bullet through his forehead.

The Final Battle

Once the Mexicans were inside the Alamo, the defenders on the walls turned their cannon around and fired inward. The Mexican Army and Texians fought in the open plaza, often with bayonets (rifles with knife blades on the end) and by hand-to-hand combat.

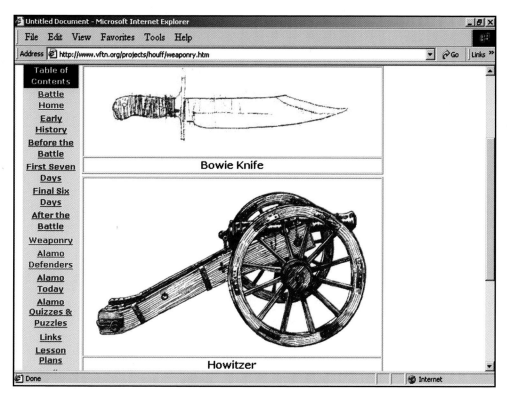

Bowie Knife

Howitzer

The bowie knife is perhaps the best-known weapon from the Battle of the Alamo. Although experts disagree over who first designed the 12-inch knife, Jim Bowie made it famous with his colorful stories. To this day, no one has found Jim Bowie's original knife.

A Houston Family Album

Sam

Margaret

The Kids

Back   Next

(936) 294-1832
contact

Sam Houston

Internet

▲ After defeating Santa Anna at the Battle of San Jacinto on April 22, 1836, Major General of the Army of the Republic of Texas Sam Houston went on to be elected president of the Republic of Texas. After Texas was annexed by the United States in 1845, Houston served as one of the state's first senators.

This was the thirteenth day of the battle, and the fighting was fierce. Some Texians tried to escape, first out of the one side of the fort, then out the other. Despite their attempts, they were all killed, many by Mexican soldiers on horseback armed with lances. A lance is a spear-like weapon with a steel tip.

Defenders retreated into the rooms along the Alamo's west wall and also inside the Long Barrack. They fired their guns through spaces in the walls and windows. Some of the most terrible fighting took place from room to room. Hospitalized in a room along the south wall, Jim Bowie was killed in his bed.[17]

The last of the fighting took place around the church—the area defended by David Crockett and his followers. The cannon that were mounted on top of the church walls fired into the Mexican attackers. This could not stop the Mexican charge. The fighting ended at 6:30 A.M.

Between five and seven Texian soldiers survived and were taken prisoner. Santa Anna was furious at that. After all, he had ordered that no prisoners be taken. The surviving soldiers were immediately executed. Even a Texian cat was killed.[18]

The few noncombatants—women, children, and slaves—had huddled in a room of the ruined church during the final battle. Of the people inside the Alamo, only they were spared.[19] Although accounts vary, as many as six hundred Mexican soldiers may have been killed or wounded in the battle.[20]

Too Little, Too Late

General Sam Houston, the leader of the Texas Revolution, was in the Texas town of Washington-on-the-Brazos when the Alamo fell. He was at a convention in which Texas declared its independence from Mexico. He was working on a treaty with the Cherokee Indians. Houston saw no need to help the Alamo's defenders. Perhaps he thought that Colonel Fannin had come to the fortress' rescue with his promised reinforcements. Or perhaps Houston simply had not taken the Mexican threat to the Alamo seriously.[21]

Unknown to the Alamo's defenders, the convention had declared independence from Mexico on March 2. So on the ninth day of the siege, Texas had become an independent nation.

On March 6, Houston finally left to help the Alamo's defenders. Sadly, they were all already dead. The ringing cry "Remember the Alamo!" would help Houston rally his troops. On April 21, 1836, Houston defeated Santa Anna's army at the Battle of San Jacinto, winning independence for Texas. Santa Anna was captured the next day. He was sent to Washington, D.C., and was eventually allowed to return to Mexico.

Legends and Living History

There are as many legends as facts about what really happened at the Alamo. Even experts on the Alamo disagree about which stories might be true. Here are a few questions that have troubled historians over the years.

▷ Did Colonel Travis Really Draw a Line in the Sand?

As the story goes, Travis drew a line in the sand with his sword. Then he asked all the men who were willing to die with him in the Alamo's defense to cross it.

That seems almost too dramatic to be true, but four survivors claimed that it actually happened. One of these was Louis Rose, the only man who did not cross the line. The other three were Enrique Esparza, a young Tejano boy; Joe, Travis's slave; and Susannah Dickinson, whose husband was killed the next day.

▷ Did Jim Bowie Die Firing Pistols From His Bed?

Jim Bowie was too ill to rise from his bed during the final attack. Certain "eyewitnesses" claimed that Bowie died with a blazing pistol in each hand. They said that Bowie killed as many Mexicans as he could—before being bayoneted to death.

Unfortunately, these witnesses were not actually in the same room as Bowie. He was probably alone with his killers when he died. Some Mexican soldiers mockingly claimed that Bowie did not resist at all. They might not have known how ill he was. Nobody really knows how Jim Bowie met his end. Yet if Bowie had any strength left at all, it seems likely that he died fighting.[1]

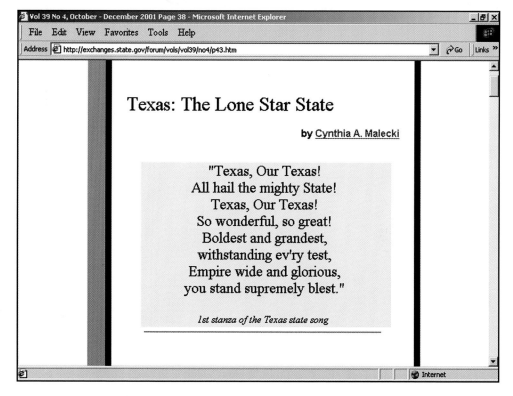

Vol 39 No 4, October - December 2001 Page 38 - Microsoft Internet Explorer

File   Edit   View   Favorites   Tools   Help

Address | http://exchanges.state.gov/forum/vols/vol39/no4/p43.htm | Go | Links »

Texas: The Lone Star State

by Cynthia A. Malecki

"Texas, Our Texas!
All hail the mighty State!
Texas, Our Texas!
So wonderful, so great!
Boldest and grandest,
withstanding ev'ry test,
Empire wide and glorious,
you stand supremely blest."

1st stanza of the Texas state song

| Internet

Texans are known to be people who are proud of the state's culture, history, and heritage. This can be seen from reading the lyrics to their state song.

What About David Crockett?

According to legend, David Crockett was killed while knocking down Mexican soldiers with the butt of his empty rifle. No one knows whether this story is true. Some witnesses claim to have seen Crockett's body near the church after the battle. The question is whether or not he died fighting.

According to some Mexican sources, Crockett was one of the defenders taken prisoner after the battle. If so, he was soon executed. Some historians doubt these accounts. Authorities strongly disagree as to how Crockett met his end.[2]

△ *These sculptures are carved into the bottom of the cenotaph, or memorial, that stands in Alamo Plaza. The two men shown here are William B. Travis (left) and David Crockett.*

▷ How Many Defenders Really Died at the Alamo?

The official list of defenders slain at the Alamo includes 189 names.[3] A growing number of historians, however, believe the list should be longer.

It is known that thirty-two volunteers arrived from Gonzales on the eighth day of the siege. They may not have been the Alamo's only reinforcements. Some sixty men from Gonzales might have arrived on the tenth day of the siege. If so, 250 or more defenders died at the Alamo.[4]

▷ Living History at the Alamo Today

Most likely, questions will always remain about exactly what happened at the Alamo. After all, no defenders survived to tell the story. Today, visitors go there to see some of the Alamo's original buildings—and consider its stories and mysteries—at Alamo Plaza in downtown San Antonio, Texas. On special occasions, staff and volunteers in costume help re-create life in the Alamo as it was in the 1800s.

The Alamo exists today because of many people's efforts. After the famous battle, Santa Anna ordered his men to level everything to the ground, but the soldiers left the walls of the church standing. Part of the Long Barrack also survived. The Alamo became United States property when Texas became a state. Over the years, it has been used by the Catholic Church, and also as a store, a military supply depot, and a warehouse.[5]

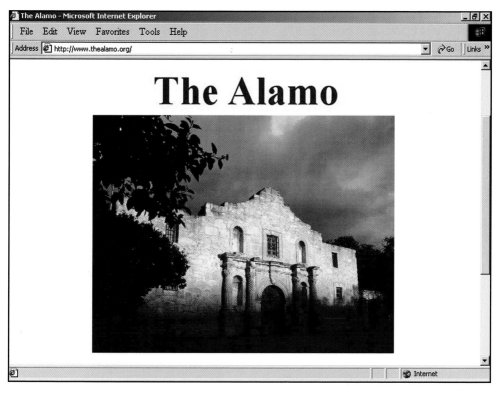

The Misión de San Antonio de Valero became known as the Alamo in the early 1800s when a Spanish cavalry unit began to name the old mission after their hometown, Alamo de Parras, Coahuila. Alamo is Spanish for "cottonwood."

This shot of the Cenotaph shows the north and west sides of the monument. The west side features the statues of Travis and Crockett. The north side features a feminine figure that represents the state of Texas. She is holding the shields of Texas and the United States.

The Daughters of the Republic of Texas

The Daughters of the Republic of Texas (DRT) was founded in 1891 to preserve historical records and encourage historical research. In 1893, the DRT made preservation of the Alamo a goal.

In the early 1900s, eighteen-year-old Clara Driscoll returned to Texas from years of study in Europe. She had seen carefully preserved historic buildings in Europe and was shocked at the poor condition of the Alamo. Clara Driscoll joined the Daughters of the Republic of Texas and worked to preserve the Alamo. She used her personal family fortune to pay part of the costs.[6]

In 1905, the Daughters of the Republic of Texas took over management of the Alamo. Today the DRT keeps the site open without charging admission.

Alamo Plaza

The city of San Antonio, which started out as Béxar, grew to encircle the Alamo. So the Alamo is now in downtown San Antonio. Alamo Plaza is smaller than the old compound, but it includes the original church and Long Barrack. The walls around the Alamo, all the pathways, the gift shop, and the library are newer. Patios and courtyards provide space for history lectures, and visitors also stroll through the beautiful Alamo Gardens.

△ *The city of San Antonio, Texas, has been built around the Alamo. The Daughters of the Republic of Texas continue to maintain the Shrine and other buildings on the premises.*

The Shrine (the church), Long Barrack Museum, and Gift Museum house exhibits about the Texas Revolution and Texas history. Recently, traces of wall paintings called frescoes were discovered in a room of the church. The paintings, which date back to the 1700s and the days of the Misión San Antonio de Valero, are being carefully preserved for visitors to enjoy.

A marble monument known as the Alamo Cenotaph stands on Alamo Plaza in front of the Alamo. Erected in 1939 by the Texas Centennial Commission, the 60-foot-tall memorial expresses the theme "Spirit of Sacrifice." Among its features are portraits of James Bowie, William B. Travis, David Crockett, and others who died at the Alamo.

Alamo Movies

Near Alamo Plaza, visitors can see an IMAX presentation of *The Price of Freedom.* This huge-screen movie re-creates the thirteen-day battle, complete with all the familiar characters.

Many other movies have been made about the Battle of the Alamo. In the 1950s, an entire Texas town was reproduced near San Antonio for a movie called *The Alamo,* starring John Wayne. The reproduction was based on old Spanish plans and built from adobe bricks created by Mexican craftsmen. The Alamo Village has since been open to visitors.

In 2004, another movie called *The Alamo* was released by Touchstone Pictures, owned by Walt Disney Studios. It stars Dennis Quaid, Billy Bob Thornton, Jason Patric, and Patrick Wilson.

Remembering the Spirit of the Alamo

The buildings, exhibits, and gardens within Alamo Plaza honor the courage of those who died there. They help us understand what happened at that heroic moment in Texan and American history. Most importantly, they show us what that time was like for those who lived it.

Glossary

adobe—Brick-like material made of sun-dried earth and straw.

annex—To add a territory to an existing political entity, such as a country or state.

artillery—Firearms such as guns and howitzers.

bayonet—A steel blade attached to a rifle that is used during hand-to-hand combat.

cavalry—A portion of an army that rides on horseback. Since horses are no longer used, today's cavalries are tank brigades.

conquistador—A leader or conqueror in the Spanish conquest of territories in the Americas.

convento—A community or house of priests.

democracy—A form of government in which the people rule through majority voting or by being represented in government by elected officials.

dictator—A person who rules with absolute power.

fresco—A painting created on a moist lime plaster with water-based pigments.

lance—A spear-like weapon with a steel tip.

mission—A place from which a religious group spreads its faith or carries out humanitarian work.

presidio—The Spanish word for a military post.

rear guard—The part of a military unit that has the job of protecting it from being attacked from behind.

republic—A form of government in which people elect their leaders.

Tejanos—People of Hispanic descent who were born or lived in Texas at the time of the Texan fight for independence.

Chapter 1. A Desperate Dash for Help

1. J. R. Edmondson, *The Alamo Story: From Early History to Current Conflicts* (Plano, Tex.: Republic of Texas Press, 2000), p. 320.

2. Reuben Rendon Lozano, as appears in Wallace L. McKeehan, "Sons of Dewitt Colony Texas: Colonel Juan N. Seguín," *Viva Tejas,* 1997–2004, <http://www.tamu.edu/ccbn/dewitt/vivatejas.htm> (May 29, 2003).

3. Ibid.

4. Edmondson, p. 320.

5. Juan Nepomuceno Seguín, *A Revolution Remembered: Memoirs & Selected Correspondence of Juan N. Seguín,* ed. Jesus de la Teja (Austin, Tex.: State House Press, 1991), pp. 107–108.

6. The Daughters of the Republic of Texas, *The Alamo Long Barrack Museum* (Dallas: Taylor Publishing Company, 1986), p. 17.

7. Edmondson, p. 324.

8. Susan Prendergast Schoelwer, "San Antonio de Valero Mission," *The Handbook of Texas Online,* December 4, 2002, <http://www.tsha.utexas.edu/handbook/online/articles/view/SS/uqs8.html> (October 27, 2003).

9. Edmondson, p. 305.

Chapter 2. Land of Many Flags

1. The Daughters of the Republic of Texas, *The Alamo: Long Barrack Museum* (Dallas: Taylor Publishing Company, 1986), p. 5.

2. Susan Prendergast Schoelwer, "San Antonio de Valero Mission," *The Handbook of Texas Online,* December 4, 2002, <http://www.tsha.utexas.edu/handbook/online/articles/view/SS/uqs8.html> (October 27, 2003).

3. Ibid.

4. J. R. Edmondson, *The Alamo Story: From Early History to Current Conflicts* (Plano, Tex.: Republic of Texas Press, 2000), p. 46.

5. Ibid., p. 27.

6. Ibid., p. 29.

7. Ibid., p. 46.

8. The University of Texas Institute of Texan Cultures at San Antonio, "The Spanish, Mexican, Tejanos," 2000, <http://www.texancultures.utsa.edu/publications/texansoneandall/tejano.htm> (October 27, 2003).

Chapter 3. Famous Soldiers

1. PageWise, Inc., "The Alamo Battle," 2001, <http://allsands.com/History/Places/thealamobattle_zzm_gn.htm> (March 19, 2004).

2. Jim Tuck, "Master of Chutzpah: The Unsinkable Antonio Lopez de Santa Anna," History of Mexico, 2001, <http://www.mexconnect.com/mex_/history/jtuck/jtsantaanna.html> (October 28, 2003).

3. J. R. Edmondson, *The Alamo Story: From Early History to Current Conflicts* (Plano, Tex.: Republic of Texas Press, 2000), p. 67.

4. Ibid., p. 79.

5. Wilfred H. Callcott, "Santa Anna, Antonio López de," *The Handbook of Texas Online,* December 4, 2002, <http://www.tsha.utexas.edu/handbook/online/articles/view/SS/fsa29.html> (October 27, 2003).

6. Edmondson, pp. 89–91.

7. William R. Williamson, "Bowie, James," *The Handbook of Texas Online,* December 4, 2002, <http://www.tsha.utexas.edu/handbook/online/articles/view/BB/fbo45.html> (October 27, 2003).

8. Edmondson, pp. 141–142.

9. Ibid, pp. 142–144.

10. Ibid., p. 263.

11. Michael A. Lofaro, "Crockett, David," *The Handbook of Texas Online,* December 4, 2002, <http://www.tsha.utexas.edu/handbook/online/articles/view/CC/fcr24.html> (October 17, 2003).

12. Edmondson, pp. 267–271.

13. Ibid., pp. 265–266.

14. Michael A. Lofaro, "Crockett, David," *The Handbook of Texas Online,* December 4, 2002, <http://www.tsha.utexas.edu/handbook/online/articles/view/CC/fcr24.html> (October 17, 2003).

15. Ibid.

16. The Daughters of the Republic of Texas, *The Alamo: Long Barrack Museum* (Dallas: Taylor Publishing Company, 1986), p. 29.

Chapter 4. The Siege and Battle of the Alamo

1. The Daughters of the Republic of Texas, *The Alamo Long Barrack Museum* (Dallas: Taylor Publishing Company, 1986), p. 38.

2. Edmondson, p. 300.

3. Ibid., p. 301.

4. The Daughters of the Republic of Texas, p. 38.

5. Edmondson, pp. 352, 357.

6. Ibid., pp. 324–327.

7. Ibid., p. 338.

8. Ibid., p. 350.

9. Ibid., p. 341.

10. Ibid., pp. 317, 331.

11. Stephen L. Hardin, "Alamo, Battle of the," *The Handbook of Texas Online,* December 4, 2002, <http://www.tsha.utexas.edu/handbook/online/articles/view/AA/qea2.html> (October 27, 2003).

12. The Daughters of the Republic of Texas, p. 41.

13. Natalie Ornish, "Rose, Louis," *The Handbook of Texas Online,* December 4, 2002, <http://www.tsha.utexas.edu/handbook/online/articles/view/RR/froav.html> (October 27, 2003).

14. Edmondson, p. 362.

15. The Daughters of the Republic of Texas, p. 39.

16. Hardin, "Alamo, Battle of the."

17. Edmondson, pp. 367–368.

18. Ibid., pp. 371–373.

19. The Daughters of the Republic of Texas, p. 42.

20. Hardin, "Alamo, Battle of the."

21. Edmondson, p. 376.

Chapter 5. Legends and Living History

1. J. R. Edmondson, *The Alamo Story: From Early History to Current Conflicts* (Plano, Tex.: Republic of Texas Press, 2000), pp. 397–399.

2. Michael Lofaro, "Crockett, David," *The Handbook of Texas Online,* December 4, 2002, <http://www.tsha.utexas.edu/handbook/online/articles/view/CC/fcr24.html> (October 17, 2003).

3. The Daughters of the Republic of Texas, pp. 44–45.

4. Edmondson, p. 352.

5. Amelia W. Williams, "Alamo," *The Handbook of Texas Online,* December 4, 2002, <http://www.tsha.utexas.edu/handbook/online/articles/view/AA/uqa1.html> (October 27, 2003).

6. Dorothy D. DeMoss, "Driscoll, Clara," *The Handbook of Texas Online,* December 4, 2002, <http://www.tsha.utexas.edu/handbook/online/articles/view/DD/fdr4.html> (October 30, 2003).

Further Reading

Alter, Judy. *Texas: A MyReportLinks.com Book.* Berkeley Heights, N.J.: MyReportLinks.com Books, 2002.

Edmondson, J. R. *Jim Bowie: Frontier Legend, Alamo Hero.* New York: PowerPlus Books, 2003.

Gunderson, Cory. *The Battle of the Alamo.* Edina, Minn.: Abdo Publishing Company, 2003.

Hoyt, Edwin P. *The Alamo: An Illustrated History.* Dallas: Taylor Publishing Company, 1999.

Levy, Janey. *The Alamo: A Primary Source History of the Legendary Texas Mission.* New York: Rosen Central Primary Source, 2003.

Marcovitz, Hal. *The Alamo.* Philadelphia: Mason Crest Publishers, 2003.

McGowen, Tom. *The Alamo.* New York: Children's Press, 2003.

Murphy, Jim. *Inside the Alamo.* New York: Delacorte Press, 2003.

Retan, Walter. *The Story of Davy Crockett: Frontier Hero.* Milwaukee: Gareth Stevens, 1997.

Sorrels, Roy. *The Alamo in American History.* Springfield, N.J.: Enslow Publishers, Inc., 1996.

Tanaka, Shelley. *A Day That Changed America: The Alamo.* New York: Hyperion Books, 2003.

Tolliver, Ruby C. *Santa Anna: Patriot or Scoundrel.* Dallas: Hendrick-Long Publishing Company, 1993.

Wade, Mary Dodson. *People of Texas.* Chicago: Heinemann Library, 2003.